MEANINGFUL THOUGHTS

BY JACK JOINER

THE WAY IT MAY VERY WELL BE

*These unorganized words are in print so that
the writer may better understand his own mind*

Sincere thoughts from his heart

Order this book online at www.trafford.com
or email orders@trafford.com

Most Trafford titles are also available at major online book retailers.

Printed in Victoria, BC, Canada.

ISBN: 978-1-4269-3116-1 (sc)
ISBN: 978-1-4269-3117-8 (e-book)

Library of Congress Control Number: 2010905922

*Our mission is to efficiently provide the world's finest, most comprehensive book publishing
service, enabling every author to experience success. To find out how to publish your
book, your way, and have it available worldwide, visit us online at www.trafford.com*

Trafford rev. 4/28/2010

www.trafford.com

North America & international
toll-free: 1 888 232 4444 (USA & Canada)
phone: 250 383 6864 ♦ fax: 812 355 4082

I am grateful that many of our officials in the government are very much concerned about the direction that our great country is heading. It should be recognized that the main ingredient, that has made our country great, is being left out. "What a disgrace in the sight of God to let our country try to operate without Him." God- fearing folks are wondering how the people that run this country could let the loud mouth atheist control them unless they are also atheists.

Let God Speak Through His People:

The loud mouths of this country appear to be in control of how we live. (The saying "the squeaking wheel gets the grease.")

Somehow or other, the way we live is getting out of the control of the people. A few of the people of this nation have gotten into control of how and whom we worship. It's no secret that they have pushed God out of schools, government and many other places. Is it a fact that the word "GOD" is becoming the big "G" word similar to some other words that we cannot mention because of being offensive????

Why are we not allowed to pray or use the word God in public gatherings?? The answer is: we, the public of this nation are sitting by and talking about it and doing little about it.

Why would it not be feasible to give the authority back to the people by placing it on the voting ballot so that the majority of the people of this nation could again be in control of how we speak, how we worship, when we worship and when we may say or print the word "GOD?"

We have procrastinated far too long and now the few of this nation and other atheist (as our adverbs) are dictating to us: when, where, how and how much!!!!

To become angry with someone just because they disagree with me is just pure ignorance on my part, because if everyone agreed with each other the world would improve very slowly if any, and may become degraded, but with disagreements, the thinking process is put into action and ideas come about.

I hope that I will always remember that my complaining makes others around me uncomfortable and only degrades my intelligence.

There are some happy people in this world, but, then there are those who complain.

Every time that I open my mouth to talk to others, I'm evaluated, labeled, judged, characterized and categorized to a position of value in their mind. I am judged by what I say, the way I speak, my body language, and my facial expressions.

Good looks, good home, good car, money in the bank and much of the world's goods is not the answer to happiness, peace with self, peace with others, and peace with God. A good ATTITUDE is necessary to have self peace and for others that you come in contact with to have peace.

The truth is not an option.

Want your words to be meaningful? Let them be few!

Most of us are self-made slaves. That is, we're slaves to self. We want more before we appreciate what we have. We always compare ourselves with others that have more than we, then try to live up to their financial standards. I, for one, know that I'd be better off, happier and more pleasant to be, with if I would stop and give God the credit for all that I call mine. Instead of complaining, I should be more thankful for what I have. I should keep my eyes on the goodness of God and what he does for me than watching the "upper-crust" and the so- called "elite" of the human race. It wouldn't hurt me a bit to get my eyes on those who are not so fortunate as I. If I'm ever going to do anything for God it would be to help fulfill the needs of others because He dwells within them as well as within me. I know that receiving is necessary for us to survive, but giving to those in need makes life worth living.

I hope that I never reach the stage of my life that I verbally pass judgment, give my opinion, and criticize almost every person, their appearance and actions. My desire is, if I cannot say something good about others, then I pray that I'll not say anything. I consider all people to be loved by God. They are His handiwork, His very own creation. Who am I that I can criticize God??? By what authority do I have to be critical of what God has done and is doing? The only one that gives that kind of authority is Satan and his angels. Do I have that kind of authority? -- Do you? - Think about it ! !

If you are at all concerned about where you will be after this life then read what Jesus has to say in the bible in Matthew 25: 31-46 and then make an evaluation of your life.

Matthew 25: 31 through 46 is a real eye opener.

I like what Mark Twain said: "I'm not disturbed by what I don't understand as I read the Bible; however, I am disturbed by what I <u>do</u> understand.

For me to dwell on a problem makes it much bigger. The more that I talk about it, the larger the problem gets. My time should be spent on finding a solution.

What is worry? Worry is doubting that God is big enough to handle my problems! Then worry is sin.

Psalms 141:3, "Set a watch, O Lord, before my mouth; keep the door of my lips."

If I have something that bothers me and I cannot do anything about it, then the problem and my worries are magnified each time that I discuss it with anyone other than my Lord.

They who try to create their own heaven on earth by trying to "out-do" the fictitious Jones's, not only create a "hell-on-earth" for themselves, but for all others around them!

I believe the old saying, "A person will not be satisfied with what they want until they appreciate what they have."

As someone said, "The hole in our moral ozone is larger than the hole in our atmospheric ozone."

If it takes more "showy things" to give some people the normal level of confidence in themselves, then lack of self-confidence may be the problem.

If you were raised in a barn, it shows when you close doors!

This sounds weird but true: EVERY STEP OF OUR LIFE HAS BROUGHT US TO THE EXACT SPOT THAT WE ARE AT THIS MOMENT.

SHORTIES:

Peace, happiness and contentment cannot
be purchased with money.
Don't judge your needs in relation to what
others have who have more than you.

Knowing that it is not natural to be content,
man ought to "re-focus" on pleasing God!

Minds that are filled with so many frivolous and
unimportant things that amount to nothing
are usually the minds of small people.

Those who consider others to be important have peace
of mind, are contented, and are "GIANTS."

With much unnecessary idle talk come
many unnecessary problems.
The more the idle talk, the more the unnecessary problems.

Some folks sacrifice their own happiness by
having to have everything their way.

Bad people are not bad all of the time and good
people are not good all the time, so, why don't we
just let it go at that and not fret over evildoers.

Human problems are greatly enlarged with excess talk.

You can always tell a wise man by the
smart things he does not say.

SOME OLDIES FROM YEARS GONE BY:

The wisest among us is a fool in some things.

Don't be afraid of opposition – remember, a
kite rises against, not with the wind.

A committee is a group of people who individually
can do nothing but who as a group can meet
and decide nothing can be done.

Pray earnestly: you can't get a thousand
dollar answer to a 10 cent prayer.

One way to save face is to keep the lower part of it shut.

Swallowing angry words is much easier than having to eat them.

Some people know how to say nothing, but few know when.

Lord help me to think by yards and speak in inches.

xxxxxxxxxxxxxxxxxx

We would all be better off if we would read the third
chapter of St. James in the Bible more often.

Suspicion always haunts the guilty mind!

More Shorts:

A person is respected or condemned by his own words.
My derogatory remarks about someone only degrade me.
My bragging on myself also degrades me.
I lift the spirit of others if I compliment them - it also helps me.
I lose many points with those whom I am verbally critical of.
I, not them, am degraded when I belittle
the attitude or actions of others.
I degrade or upgrade myself every time
that I say something to someone.
If I speak well of someone it upgrades them and me.
If I speak badly of someone it degrades us both.
What a waste, when a person does not make the best
of his God-given time on earth.   [think about it]
Lord, what do You want to do, in me?
He who speaks all of his mind all of the time is a babbler and
makes life very uncomfortable for all who have to listen.
Are you happy or sad because of my presence?
Are you happier to see me approaching or are you happier when
I am leaving? I hope that I will always be sensitive to this.

What is worse than the blind trying to lead the blind?
ans: The blind trying to lead those who can see the way plainly!

When a person is degrading someone who is not present,
they're only degrading them self, in my opinion.

It appears to me that the folks who feel sorry for themselves, are
the people that do the most complaining. Complaining causes
more unhappiness for others than any one thing that I know.

Sometimes it seems as if every one of us is trying
to make ourselves the victim in each circumstance
so that we may have the pity of our audience!

If you observe a person gossiping, tearing down
another's character, and saying all manner of unfavorable
things about them: know for a fact, that they will
do the same with you when you're not around.

We are not necessarily born equal, we are born with
equal rights. After birth it is the responsibility of each
individual to earn his or her own rights. Things that
are given to us are not our rights. Welfare money and
foods, etc., <u>are not rights!</u> The only rights that we
have are essentially earned by each individual.

Others know us by what we do with what we have.

Attempting to control others takes away much happiness in
a person's life, much less the unhappiness it causes others.

There is pleasure in receiving, but there is more
pleasure derived from what a person gives.

God gives to us according to our ability to receive it. He
does not give to us beyond our capabilities. He gives us the
ability to control our own <u>attitude.</u> He also gives us the ability
to control our own <u>patience,</u> therefore, He is giving us the
ability to control the things that are absolutely necessary
to have good health and a happy life. It is a pleasure to be
with people who are patient and have a good attitude!

Big people get upset with big problems, Little
people get upset with little problems.
A person is only as big as the things that upset them.

The more love that one has for himself, the more unhappy
he is, even to the extent of damaging his health.

If people are totally in the will of God, their conversation will
reflect love and compassion for others. However, if people
are unknowingly guided by Satan, then their conversation
will reflect envy, hate, jealousy or the desire to degrade
others, while regarding themselves in very high esteem.

PESSIMIST: * looks for things bad-
                 * searches for things to worry about-
                 * is filled with <u>gloom & doom</u>-
                 * looks for the bad side of people

Blaming others is the work of Satan.

OPTIMIST: * looks for the things that are good-
                 * searches for the bright side of life-
                 * is filled with sunshine-
                 * looks for the good in people

Compliment others who are worthy, it will have uplifting effects
on them and you.

You cannot be satisfied with others until you're satisfied with
yourself.
You cannot even be happy until you're satisfied with yourself.

The value of a favor to me is a total loss if one complains about
having to do it.

Friends do not complain about the privilege of helping each
other.

Don't make a big issue out of your efforts to do a favor for me.

If you can't be friendly to me, don't be anything to me.

Don't be critical of the way that I do a thing, until you know of a better way.

I also wonder if folks who have to listen to radio, tv, or some useless babbling most of the time are trying to avoid receiving the message of the direction for their lives that their mind is receiving from the Holy Spirit.

I think that people who want to be true to themselves will attempt to avoid all distractions such as excessive junk sounds, loud secular music, idle talk and other vanities which tend to over-ride the voice of our creator.

If a person is not receiving direction from the Holy Spirit, I wonder who or what is standing in the way.

It is much harder listening to nothing being said than it is for the one saying it. The speaker is evidently receiving mental therapy, but it sure places a heavy burden on the very heart of the listener.

Luke 12:15 - "A man's life consists not in the abundance of the things which he possesses."

My belief is that God judges me by the ways that I use the resources that he has provided me with!

One can have power or self-pity, but one cannot have both.
Having self-pity borders on being stupid.
Satan does not like joy. He likes depression, self-pity and disease.

To act like the devil nowadays is accepted.

To act like God is not the acceptable thing in this day and time. Grieving over past mistakes destroys one's joy and happiness, both present and future.

I should never take this lightly: "I will be judged on what I do with what I have."

The people who talk excessively are trying hard to promote themselves, without regard to the person(s) having to listen. They do not know that they're not promoting themselves in the eyes of the listener, but are demoting themselves.

The people who gossip about others are COWARDS.

Folks who do all of their thinking out loud are a tremendous burden on others. It surpasses boredom!

People who are concerned about themselves only, and with little thought given about the good of others, are selfish and are very unhappy and unstable.

Those who serve God by ministering to others find happiness and peace with Him.

Others determine what type of person you are by your talk. They are impressed or *un*-impressed by what you say and how you say it.

Many folks degrade themselves by trying to impress others.

Pretty is as pretty does.

As a bottle of water placed in a refrigerated area, so is a person placed in a certain environment; each becomes as its surroundings.

It appears that people who constantly complain, placing blame, and who see only bad and nothing good in others have a problem staying in the sovereign will of God!!!

I feel sorry for people who can only see that which they can find fault with - it's a terrific handicap to not be able to see good instead of bad. Unless they change, they'll go to their graves never knowing how to appreciate the many good things and people that God has blessed them with.

What do you feel about people who constantly complain? My thoughts are that that they believe that they have missed something along the way, and are lacking in confidence.

Usually unsolicited opinions are worth just exactly what they cost.

Now listen, people who exaggerate the truth do not fall short of lying.

People who do not keep their word, LIE!

Those who are always late for appointments fall short of being totally honest, and show very little respect for those who are kept waiting.

Folks who are continually trying to impress others by putting on a false front only end up depressing themselves.

Our lives are like the ocean waves, the wind, and the temperature: sometimes we're up and sometimes we're down.

Our activities describe our faith. As our faith is, so goes our life. Our lifestyle describes our faith. We live what we really believe.

The very, very worst thing that could ever happen to me is that, the once-in-a-lifetime thing happens, <u>I WAKE UP IN HELL!!</u> (think about it).
Just one glimpse of hell, and I'd never go there!

It is good that people join the church because it is a good place to hear the Gospel; however, it's sad if they're misled into thinking that they will be saved by church membership and without a personal relationship with the Lord. Conviction, Godly sorrow for past sins, and repentance are essential for salvation, believe it or not! Professing without possessing is one way of taking the name of the Lord in vain!

You're not talking to the right person when you're talking continuously, non-stop to me about how everybody mistreats you and how you have more troubles than anyone else. You need to be talking this over with THE ONE that can help you.

You're not helping others when you're laying all of your aches, pains and problems on them. You're not making them have a desire to be in your presence.

My complaining is evidence of my not having everything my way. I have to make a choice; "Do I want to have friends, or, do I have to have everything my way?" The truth is that I cannot have both!!!

There are folks who spend a lot of their time in attempting to promote themselves and demote others. I think that they have it in reverse. If they put forth their efforts on promoting others, then they would be promoted in the eyes of others. It's a shame that they waste a large portion of their lives and happiness in worrying about what others think of them.

To compliment others and to help fulfill their needs will make a person be highly thought of. It's like a smile, you get more back than you put in, or a mirror, you get back the very same thing that you put in. A smile is like a good investment, almost all time you get back a good return for your efforts.

It is necessary that when a person gives another a compliment, that they also have a good countenance to support it.

Sometimes I think that I'm prone to let vanity take preference over convenience. (I'm probably not the only one that does that.)

I'm Uncomfortable In
The Presence Of:

1. Opinionated people
2. Judgmental people
3. Gossiping people
4. People who try too hard to impress.
5. Folks who "talk down" to me.
6. Those who see only my faults.
7. Those who have nothing to say but say it anyway.
8. Those who tell me all of their personal problems every time we meet.
9. Those who place blame.
10. Those who glory in destroying the reputation of others.
11. Those who blame the innocent.
12. People who invent personal degradation against others.
13. Those who are my "adverbs" - always telling me when, where, how and how much.
14. People who interrupt, without good cause. (what I gather from this is that they think that what they have to say is far more important than what I was saying.)
15. Those who pry into the personal affairs of others.
16. Contrary and argumentative people.
17. Habitual complainers.
18. Folks with negative attitudes.
19. Pessimists
20. Those who are slack in carrying their end of the load.
21. Sneaky type people.
22. People with halitosis.

23. Hypocrites.
24. Liars.
25. Those who think that they are far superior to me. By their attitude and talk, I can detect it.
26. Those who feel sorry for themselves without good cause.
27. People who are impatient; (If hens were impatient, there would be no baby chicks.)
28. People who speak their opinionated conclusions before I finish what I'm going to say.
29. Those who insist on having their way even at the risk of losing a friend.

I Like Being In The Presence Of:

1. The Holy Spirit.
2. Those who uphold the good character of others.
3. Folks who are always just what they are.
4. People who give credit where credit is due.
5. Those who respect the opinions of others.
6. People who have a positive attitude.
7. People who are optimists.
8. People who like to do more than is expected of them.

Have you ever seen folks who appear to think that everything and everybody are in orbit around them, and think that they're the center of all creation?

We all like to have our way with everything; however, some go to great extremes to have things their way, even to the extent of someone else's hurt and [or] expense.

Think about this: "When you win, normally, somebody loses!"

I must forgive all others before God can forgive me.

A forgiving heart is necessary for a healthy body.

Folks with "normal common sense" usually already know most things that others are telling them. They really don't need to be told over and over. When people say the same things over and over again to normal folks, it makes one believe that the one doing the repetitious talking is of questionable mentality.

Have you ever had the thought that the reason we have freedom of speech is that there are some folks that could never afford to pay for all that they say?

Much talk -- many problems

Again, have you ever thought of the fact that every thing that we say in this life, we will have to pay for, or be rewarded for in the hereafter? Therefore, there is really no free speech, you <u>will</u> have to pay for, or be paid for, everything you say. (Makes me wonder if the bookkeeping of my life is going to balance out?)

I am of the opinion that about the rudest thing that a person can do is scream at another person just because they are not feeling good, yet the person that is being screamed at has not done anything except be in their presence. It seems to me that a person that is not feeling up to par would have a good attitude instead of a bad one if they want any sympathy and attention. It is hard for me to try to help someone who is complaining about me and thinks that everything that I do is bad. I think that you cannot like someone and talk against them all the time.

When a person speaks to you in a loving and caring voice, regardless of the situation, you know instantly that it's of God. However, when a person speaks to you with hate or undeserving criticism, just consider it as Satan doing what he does best, *"Giving You Hell."*

Sometimes it appears that there are many people that are their own God, and that without their own knowledge.

If folks continually dwell on their problems, they forfeit their joy and happiness and are failing to focus on their many blessings.

Again, I cannot over emphasize enough that if a person likes someone, then they will not speak badly about them. Also, it is very easy to speak evil of those that you hate, and hard to speak bad things about those that you care about. It's easy to find good things about those you care about and easy to find bad things to say about those that you do not like. But I say don't talk about anybody, anytime, unless you can speak well of them. Remember, they are God's handiwork, and to speak evil of others is to speak evil of God. *Think about it!*

I believe that the person that makes slurry remarks about another person without their presence is not completely in the will of Almighty God.

It is impossible to be happy if you have a negative mind all the time. On the other hand, it is impossible for an optimist to be unhappy all the time. Don't you just like to be around folks who have a positive outlook on life?

Happiness comes from your own personal thoughts. Happiness comes from within one's self. <u>Don't depend on others for your own happiness!</u>

Good thoughts, peace of mind, and happiness comes from God to you. The opposite comes to you from some other source!

I can't help but feel sorry for people who speak their whole mind all the time; but, my heart goes out to those who have to listen to it.

What is love? I think that there are several kinds of what is currently referred to as love. The most common thing in modern day thinking is a love of physical and sexual attraction. Another kind of love comes about because you honor and respect another's character and attributes, which causes you to love them with the love of the Lord.

If you like a person and have things in common with them, you'll try to spend a lot of time with them. If you don't care for a person and don't have much in common with them, you'll try to avoid spending a lot of time together.
If you truly love someone, you'll overlook their insignificant faults and mistakes.

A person who is inconsiderate and likes himself better than he likes others is a very unhappy person.

It's not what you receive that brings happiness, but it's what you give. Giving without receiving has much honor; giving because you received has little honor.

When you boast about your good deeds, you have no rewards for them. You are greatly rewarded for your good deeds done in secret.

No God - no peace; know God - know peace!

I cannot do all the talking and do all the learning. I cannot do all the learning and do all the talking at the same time.

I can have more credibility with others if I remember to call their name every time I come in contact with them and to let them express themselves completely without interruption. In normal conversation, the patient listener has more credibility than the person doing all the talking.

Again, remember there is no free speech, a person will have to pay for it now or in the hereafter.

I find it difficult to give credibility to people for their good deeds if they display a very bad attitude.

I hope that I never get too preoccupied with things that hinder me from finding time to stop, be still, and listen for the Holy Spirit to speak to me. I find it almost impossible for me to hear the Holy Spirit when there is idle conversation, loud TV or radio, ball game or other unnecessary loud activities taking place.

There are two kinds of people, one who accepts and one who blames.

The true picture can be distorted by words without knowledge.

It appears that folks who tell all their personal problems and complaints are seeking pity from others. Also, people who are sincerely looking for comfort and a way to solve their problems, tell them all to God.

Do some folks think that the "here and now" is everything?

I like good fellowship and conversation as well as the next person, but God can do a good job of carrying your burdens, and I cannot.

Many times some folks are offended at the truth if it's not in their favor.

The extent of one's peace of mind and happiness is directly related to the depth of relationship a person has with God, and not because of their material possessions.

Have you ever had the experience of someone trying to interrupt you while you were talking and they would get louder and louder until you had to stop? [Irritating, isn't it.]

It's fairly difficult to enlighten those who already know everything. Like the old saying: "You can tell 'em, but you can't tell 'em much."

Some folks have a beautiful, colorful personality; then there are those whose personality is only in black and white.

By the way, did you ever dream in color? If you don't remember, then you didn't.

I hope that I never get too preoccupied with things which hinder me from finding time to stop, be still, and listen to the Holy Spirit.

I think that psychiatrists are right in advising their patients to not hold in the things that trouble them, but to let it out; tell someone about what's troubling them. The big mistake is not telling them that the only one that they can tell that is capable of helping them is God. Another human does not have the power to fulfill the need; so, why burden them beyond what they can bear? God wants the troubles laid on Him, it's a part of showing faith in Him, and a part of His plan. It's not a burden on Him, but it's showing Him that you are depending on Him. It's a means of worshiping Him. The sooner a person is able to talk to God in private about every small or large thing in his life, the sooner he will be restored to his normal self.

Proverbs: 29:11, "A fool uttereth all his mind; a wise man keepeth it in until afterwards."

Fools are known as what they are.

If a person talks their problems out with God, there is no reason to burden another human being with all their troubles.

He that is quick to anger may not have good self-control.

I just wonder if when I lose my temper, is that of God? Is that characteristic of my Lord? Could it be of Satan? Then I decide that it's not of God and it is of Satan! Could I have let Satan slither in and take charge of me and my actions without my knowledge? The answer is "yes," for when I lose my cool, Satan takes charge of my actions and my emotions. Then God is no longer running my life, but I'm completely under the control of Satan.

If you're uncomfortable in the presence of certain people, then they also will become uncomfortable with you!

As the Christian gains more faith in God; he gains more confidence in self because the Spirit of God is the Spirit that is in him.

If you show affection, you'll receive affection. If you make yourself loveable, you'll be loved. Make yourself trustworthy and you'll be trusted.

If you appear to be a slob, you will be thought of as a slob.

Atheists are not the only ones that are on their way to hell; lost believers are just as lost as atheists.

Freedom is not free!

Punishment for lost church members may be more severe because they know about the Lord, but fail to seek Him out in a personal way and fully surrender to Him.

I believe that some who take the name of Christ do so in vain. They ignore the convicting power of the Holy Spirit and will not repent, surrender, and commit their lives to Him. They just console their conscience by telling themselves that they "believe" and [or] belong to the church. You know, the devil believes and trembles.

I interpret the commandment "Thou shalt not take the Lord's name in vain," to mean to call one's self a Christian and not be obedient.

People love you for what you are and not what you pretend to be.

It is a very unhappy people who keep their mind and conversation on their own selfish desires and needs, without any thought of the needs of those around them.

I would be most miserable if I concentrated on the things that I want and don't have, rather than appreciating and enjoying the many things and privileges that I have.

If a person with a mental or physical problem understands their condition, then they can be helped. However, if they refuse to believe their condition, then they will remain a problem for themselves and those around them.

I am upgraded or degraded by those that I continuously associate with.

The things that I do for myself do not bring me happiness and satisfaction; but, satisfaction and joy comes from the things that I do for others. For me to do harm to someone else poisons the very heart of me and causes me grief that just won't go away. I should be judged by the good that I do, or would do for others, and not what I do for myself.

I am of the opinion that a person will never be healed of physical ailments with prescription or non-prescription medicines, as long as they have a slandering tongue and an unforgiving heart.

It is very uncomfortable to be with those who are "dogmatic"- that is, asserting opinions with arrogance.

It seems that lots of times we are blinded by what we don't have, to the extent that we can't see and appreciate that with which we are blessed. If you speak to a person in a pleasing manner, normally you'll get a pleasant reply. Somewhat like a mirror, what you put in it is what you get out of it.

Don't discredit yourself by talking too much.

Being the loudest doesn't make it the "rightest."

Do you ever feel like someone is using you as a "chopping-block" to lay all of their enemies and problems on while they verbally cut them up into little pieces?

He who has a foul mouth has a foul soul.

It doesn't make sense to have a clean house and have a dirty mind.

The inner person is reflected by expressions and words of the outer person.

I stress again, the tongue is an index to the mind.

Dirty mouth, dirty soul.

The tongue describes the very heart of a person.

The quality of one's life depends entirely on the god he worships.

Adverb Us Type Of Thinking

Am I <u>what</u> I would like to be?
Am I <u>where</u> I would like to be?
Am I <u>how</u> I would like to be?
If not, <u>when</u> would I like to be, <u>where</u> I would like to
be, <u>what</u> I would like to be, <u>how</u> I would like to be?

Now, and only now, can I do anything about it! Yesterday is history and cannot be reformed. Tomorrow is not in my power and shall never be, because tomorrow is always tomorrow!

People who pass judgment on everything that I do or say are very unpopular with me.

Normally in conversations, the value of a person's words is directly related to the quantity of words being spoken.

People who have a humble spirit will listen to common reasoning.

Folks who have a critical spirit will always find something wrong with things and other people that they don't care for.

I have no room in my life for a contentious person.

A rebellious person is always a thorn in the flesh for me.

It is a pleasure to be in the company of clean humorous people.

A person that finds fault in every thing and everybody is mentally ill. I wonder if the degree of a person's sickness could be determined by the percentage of the conversation that is fault finding.

Hey friend, I'll help you run my life if you want me to!

My spiritual strength is directly related to the amount of time I spend studying God's word and meditating on God in His fullness with all His attributes; also, prayer and Christian fellowship.

Even when I'm right, it would be a very rude imposition for me to impose my opinions on others.

There was once a very simple word that I liked and appreciated. That word was "honesty" - I don't see it in its true form much anymore, but I still like it.

Normally, people who talk mostly about bad things are unhappy and unpleasant. On the other hand, people who talk about good things are usually happy and pleasant to be with.

Have you ever noticed in some folk's conversation that the degrading of others and the upgrading of themselves is obvious?

Normally a person thinks that everything that he does is right, until he is blessed with a short moment of seeing himself as God sees him.

Remember, the folks that *didn't* vote had the power to reverse the election results.

I think that as humans, we often think that if we could find someone or something to blame things on, then our conscience would be cleared.

Some people are their own secret admirers.
If, in the eyes of others, it's a scam and if I'm involved in it, then I am categorized as somewhat dishonest. In their eyes I have degraded myself.

I should examine myself frequently to see if I'm honest with myself or am I an ostrich type person. Do I want others to speak the truth to me or do I want them to tell me only what I want to hear? Do I hide my head in the sand when the truth is spoken or can I face it with strength, suffer the consequences, and get up and overcome my shortcomings?

Do I have no sympathy for others if they don't do it my way? How considerate am I to others if they don't do it my way?

Sometimes we try to explain away our faults and attempt to justify our wrongs.

I wonder if there is anyone in the world who enjoys hearing folks complaining about small frivolous things.

Have you ever heard someone apologize and immediately say, "but I was right?" What does that do for you?

I hope that I never have so much love for myself that I cannot love others also.

I hope that I can always see myself just as I am, and not just the way that I want others to think that I am.

Only very few times in my life have I come to my senses and seen myself just as I am.

Sometimes I think that I have the personality of a rope, in that when I'm pushed, I perform very poorly. However, I can be lead fairly well.

Normally a person gets all of the attention that he deserves. [think about it]

We go to a medical physician to let him tell us what to do, then we desperately try to follow his instructions to maintain good physical health. Why then do we attend spiritual services to be instructed on how to be strong spiritually and then do not heed God's Word? By this, it is concluded that we place more value on our "temporary" physical being than we do on our eternal spiritual life, our very own soul!

It is wrong that all people should be treated equal; some are more deserving than others.

Enough is enough, and is bordering on too much!

99% of a goal is failure!

Don't engage in conversation that belittles yourself or any other person.

I hope that I'm never guilty of passing judgment without knowing all the facts.

The way I see it, low class people are classed as such because of their low morals and character, and sub-standard mind, emotions and will. It has nothing to do with their accumulated wealth!

Things _to_ step on: steps, floors, sidewalks and the ground.
Things _not_ to step on: people and the word of God.

When I worry, I'm telling God that He is not big enough to take care of my problems.

Some who have accumulated an overabundance of earthly wealth have a battitude, [my own coining of the words "bad attitude"] overgrown ego, and a disrespect for others, leads me to believe that Satan may be smiling on them!

Hear me out before you go off on a "song and dance" spree of verbal judgment.

You can know all that some people are thinking because they speak everything that they think.

To be loved you must make yourself lovable.
To get attention you must give attention to others.
You cannot "fuss" others into liking you.
Show them that you like them and they'll display a liking for you.
Your own actions will always reflect back to you.
Show consideration to others, they'll reflect more back to you.
Life is similar to a mirror, what you put in is what you get in return. However, unlike the mirror, you usually get in return more of the same of what you gave.

ADVERBS: tells you when, where, how, and how much; the method, the location, the amount and the time.
Have you ever known any people that you would class as adverbs?
Adverbs are not the most desirable people to be with.
I wonder if adverbs ever change to verbs. I think verbs would be pleasant to be around.
I am most uncomfortable in the company of adverbs.
Adverbs are not considerate of the feelings of other people.
I believe that they feel that they know more than the people around them.
Then too, adverbs could just have an inferiority complex.
Those who are continuously playing the part of an adverb are very boring to be around.

It takes longer for a mental wound to heal than it does for a physical wound. A laceration can be sewn up by a doctor and in time it will most likely heal. Words can wound to the extent that an apology cannot heal for a longer period of time, or maybe never.

A stab in the heart with words may kill your respect for the perpetrator.

I am offended by someone who apologizes for the same action repeatedly. I would rather not have an apology from someone that I know will do the same thing again. After a few times with the same offense, I find it difficult to give the apology much credit. If a person is right, then I don't want them to apologize for anything.

If you're listening then you're learning; if you're talking you're not.

Being moderate in all things creates a friendly and pleasant atmosphere.

Being "flimflam" and going to extremes keeps those about you on edge and nervous.

Being solid in all your actions gives your loved ones a secure feeling.

Your general outlook on life has a terrific impact on those who are closest to you.

Being 21 years old does not make you a man. If you're a man, you don't have to tell it, people will know it!

Being solid and stable is not accomplished by an excessive amount of words. Too much idle conversation may denote instability or an inferiority complex.

If you're not one, then don't let your appearance and actions make folks think that you are. If you appear as a certain type, you shall be known as that.

Trying to make people think that they're rich keeps lot of people in the poor house.

Knowledge is great, but wisdom is a blessing.

I may not know the need for criticism, but I can depend on it always being there.

By looking down, you can always see the upper crust.

The loafing class of people is in style. The working people are almost a thing of the past. Loafers are rewarded more now than workers were in yesteryears. Liars are plentiful, rouges are not scorned. Real Christians have no place among the average groups. Man's conscience no longer dictates that he earn his wages with work that he was hired to do. Man no longer cares or is concerned for his neighbor. Friendship is now sold for measly amounts of money.

I wonder how many would sell the lives of a million others at one dollar each, in order to become a millionaire.

May I always strive to attain the things that I can take with me, rather than the things that I cannot!

Money is easier to make than loyal friends. Effort has to be made to hold on to money, and effort has to be made to hold on to friends.

Money has to be earned; friends have to be earned. To me, friends are more valuable than an excessive amount of money.

Generally, it's hard to rise above the example that you set. You seldom are more than the life that you reflect. It is also difficult for others to respect you above the level of respect that you display for yourself.

A person that just has to "tell someone off" before he can calm down is motivated by Satan. Some folks are ready to "jump down another's throat" just by their own self-motivated frenzies.

Junk television programs frame the minds of their audience. If junk goes in, junk comes out.

I try to avoid being in the presence of opinionated people for long periods of time. By the way, the meaning of dogmatism is asserting opinions with arrogance. Dogmatics and judgmentals are not my most favorite folks.

The first impression may be made by appearance, but the lasting impression is made by the soul. [the soul being the mind, emotion and the will]. The tongue presents a picture of the soul.

I don't want to be in the presence of someone slandering another person; that person is God's handiwork, though their actions may not be.

The tyrant dies and his rule ends; the martyr dies and his rule begins.

Anyone can step on a person when he's down, but who will give him a helping hand?

Some may think that they go up a cut by cutting someone else down.

I like what Ralph Waldo Emerson said: "What you do speaks so loudly that I cannot hear what you say."

Pride ushers in destruction.

****

Unless you're warning me to beware, don't tell me about the faults of others, because I may believe that you would also gossip about me when I'm not present!

If I should walk away while someone is still talking, it should signify my disinterest in what they're saying. Why should I be compelled to listen to someone's boring, idle talk and gossip? I wonder if nature would have done mankind a favor by turning him green for a few moments when he's being bored by someone's loose lips, just to signify to the speaker that "I've had it with you, Buster."

How can a stranger to the Lord sing praises to Him? Also can a person have Christian fellowship with others if he is a stranger to the Lord?

Punctuality: Being considerate of others and their time.

Proverbs 5:3 A fool's voice is known by a multitude of words.

Butchering another person's character is almost like mental murder.

When I become a number and no longer am considered a personality, then it's my time to find another place to be.

Did you ever have to deal with the "ME FIRST" type people? Wouldn't you just like to see them go by the way of the Cross?

I would like for my home to always be a place of peace and satisfaction. I would like for it to be a place of joy, planning, happiness, laughter and peace, yet serious as the occasion requires.

I work by natural reflexes only when there is no excessive loud talking and other noises. Only a robot can perform accurately and satisfactory with excessive noise and activity present. However, the brain behind the making of the robot had to have patience, quietness and low activity present while programming it.

When I'm alone and quiet, I am entertained and find joy in listening as my mind is being spoken to in thought language.

The power of a person's words is diluted or strengthened in direct proportion to the quantity of talk that it takes to convey a message. The total of a person's words has one exact value.

By spending your time dwelling on my fallibility and your infallibility, you may never come to realize the true value of either of us!

When you're listening to radio or watching television and trying to carry on a conversation simultaneously, then you're not doing a satisfactory job at either!

My mind is not my own while watching television, it is being directed by a source other than my soul. I cannot do any creative thinking with a loudly playing television or radio on.

Some people would rather have everything their way than to have friends!

Some people have tongues that are sharper than their minds.

Have you ever seen people who would rather hear what they have to say than to allow others to talk?

Some speak with deeds, others speak with words.

I say that the people who do not appreciate that which they have are very unhappy.

Those who consider the needs of their loved ones before their own are, in most cases, happy, content, and have peace of mind.

In order to receive, you have to give. Normally I need to have a giving and for-giving heart before I appreciate that which I receive.

ODD TYPES OF THOUGHTS RUN THROUGH THE MIND:

- We all wonder about the whys....
- We are given all that we need to know, maybe not all we want to know.
- These are God's activities from "was, to is, to will be."
- Would life be enjoyable without our ups and downs?
- Suppose I decided to turn away from God, to whom would I turn?
- Would life be enjoyable without God?
- Would life even be, without God?
- Where would we be without God?

- Knowledge is unlimited just like time, space and size.
- Is God more concerned with his individual large creatures than He is with his very small microscopic creatures? Our scientists with their large telescopes are looking for large distant objects, and with their microscopes they are looking for close smaller things. It has been said that objects and creatures go in the direction of being smaller as far as they can go in the direction of being larger. In other words is size infinity, both small and large.?!?

- Questions: If you cut an apple in half, how many times could you cut the pieces in half? Would you ever finish?

Things that amaze me:
- infinity to infinity of space.....
- ever being to ever lasting......

- infinity to infinity of density......
- infinity to infinity of size......
- scientists say that minute particles of a piece of steel don't even touch.....they orbit around each other.....
- If a steel shaft is rotating about its axis, is dead center turning? Think about it, if it's turning, it's not dead center.
- We should be continuously concerned with our relationship with God and His greatness.

[now, enough of this type thinking, so we go on]

If I'm not loved by you, it's not your fault. I have to present myself lovable before I will be loved.
You cannot make yourself love me. It is entirely up to me to make myself desirable to you before you can love me.
I will have to present myself before you as desirable because of my personality, mentality, habits, hygiene, physical attraction and trustworthiness.
To be lacking in any one of the above, could damage our relationship severely.

1. personality: attitude is very important.
2. mentality: you don't have to be a genius to be loved.
3. habits: self-explanatory.
4. hygiene: very important.
5. trustworthiness: the lack of this would most definitely hinder a relationship.
6. physical attraction: [pretty or not] beauty is important, but least important of these five qualities.

We Each Put A Price Tag On Ourselves:

We tell others what we are:
1. by our stature
2. by the way we dress
3. by our patience
4. by our hygiene
5. by our walk
6. by the subjects that we choose to talk about
7. by our facial expressions [our countenance]
8. by our body language
9. by our overall appearance
10. by our self-confidence
11. by our actions
12. by our honesty
13. by our attitude
14. by the level of our conversation
15. by the quantity of idle words
16. by the quality of words we use
17. by the company we keep

We are respected by others, judged on some of the above.

If one does not crawl before he walks, his life's foundation may not be solid.

I guess that we all feel like no one has problems like we do.

Some folks seem to have more pains than anyone else; if you don't believe it, just greet them with a "HOW DO YOU DO TODAY?" If you were a doctor you'd immediately have a patient on your hands.

That which comes out of a container is that which was in it. For instance, when a person speaks a word that is not clean and says, "oh, excuse me, I should not have said that in your presence." My thought is, if it was not in you, it could not have come out!

The attitude or spirit in which something is said has more to do with the affects than what is said.

When one boast to someone else about something they've done, I think that they lose their reward for what they have done.

Tale-bearers are satanically motivated.

Consider others before you start your verbal therapy.
If you have something to say, say it, if not, don't say it.
Continuous talk is seldom heard, seldom talk is continuously heard.
Give others a chance to exercise their own brain.

Those who are headed to hell are not worried about it.
Like some atheist once said, "God knows that I don't believe in Him."

Those who are always finding fault with others are just trying to cover their own.

When someone is talking entirely too much, do you just want to ask them these questions:
    are you too nervous?
    do you think that I really want to hear this?
    do you need to dominate my mind?
    is your mouth hung in gear?
    do you think that I don't have a mind of my own?
    are you doing this just to interrupt my train of thought?
    [maybe I'm just being ornery by thinking like this.]

It Seems To Me That:

I should use what I have learned rather than study all time.
That sin ought to appear as sin!
He who talk all the time say the least.
Those who listen little are those who talk big.
Others listen very little to those who talk all the time.
Some must think that I need to be continually
entertained with their excessive idle talk.
If silence was golden, some people would be paupers.

Show me a person who, on their death bed, says, "At least I did everything my way;" and I'll show you a person who, not only lived a miserable life, but who made all others around them miserable!

He who has no time for others, has no real friends.
He who speaks all of his mind all the time, has no feeling for others!
Just because it has been said doesn't necessarily mean that it's true.
Those who love each other will have time for each other.
If you love yourself more than you love anyone else, then you will always put your needs, desires, and yourself ahead of all others.
Those who require all others to alter their plans just so that they can have things their way, are self-centered.
Those who are impatient with everyone else may be lacking in friends, or something.
You'll always have time and consideration for someone you love.
By getting louder and louder during conversation just to drown out those who are trying to talk may mean that something is about to be said that you don't want to be said. It certainly denotes an uncultivated attitude and personality, and shows disrespect for others. The picture that the audience gets is of a very selfish and inconsiderate person. The same can be said for those who

constantly interrupt, to the extent that what is intended to be relayed never gets said. These are the same ones that hear a matter later and become "out-of-sorts" because no one has told the thing to them before.

If we disagree, it doesn't mean that I'm right! It may not mean that I'm wrong though.
Getting boisterous doesn't gain any righteousness. Getting loud doesn't make it right.
Talking on top of some one's conversation doesn't make it right. Out-talking your opponent doesn't mean you're right, nor does it make you a friend!
I'm in the habit of saying "win an argument, lose a friend."

Again, let me say, I'm not offended by folks who were raised in barns, only those who continue to slam doors.

Verbalist: one who favors words over ideas or facts.
Loquacious: very talkative Garrulous: habitually talkative

It has been said that everything that we do is because of fear of punishment or hope of reward or both.
Some want their share of the pie without their share of the problems.

Not only is the brain a transformer, it is also a receiver and transmitter.
The only time that is, is right now! That which was is past and is not.
That which is yet to come is not.

To have eyes only for that which you cannot afford brings depreciation in you for that which you already have, and causes depression and anxiety.

I like to be with folks who don't find fault, don't ever complain, don't ever make statements that discredit others and who really appreciate nature and that which the Lord has blessed them with. [That's the positive side of the coin, I'm sure you can understand what the flip side is.]

I'd rather be feeling a little pain than nothing at all.

A person who is concerned only with his own needs live a very unhappy life. They also don't make it too comfortable for those around them. One cannot see the needs of others when their only concern is with self wants.

Live your own life and thoughts, not the "store bought" thoughts and lives of people on television, radio, and the idle minds of the secular world. That which you listen to and watch on television molds your life in their direction, because the sum of all of your thoughts is what you really are.

Your influence with me is governed by your attitude toward me and not by anything else. Your <u>attitude</u> toward me, and not my fear of punishment or hope of reward, will govern your influence with me.
Your influence with me should be directly related to your affection for me! Normally, a person is rewarded for their dedicated efforts and accomplishments in filling the needs of others. A person should be rewarded by others according to their attitude and personal affection shown to them.

There is peace to to found in seasons of silence.

It is a very tiring thing to be the captivated audience of someone performing their mental therapy of condemnation, gossip and other small talk for long periods of time. It is my thinking that Satan is speaking through those who are always gossiping and condemning other people. I believe that I should never say anything about a person that I would not say in their presence, unless it is a compliment and may embarrass them in the presence of others.

I believe that I should never interrupt another's train of thought in conversation except it be an emergency, or they were getting out of line with their idle talking. I believe in being a good listener to the right type of speaker.

You'll probably never know what I would have said, unless you had not monopolized the conversation. A person that rambles on and on with their idle words probably has a feeling of inferiority.

It is a very uncomfortable situation to be in, in the company of a constant complainer. It's time that I do some serious soul searching of myself when I am complaining about everything and everybody.
He who constantly criticizes others, does so because he feels less than others and hopes to better himself by putting others down!

Sometimes man is never satisfied or thankful for what he has; the more he has, the more he wants and lot of times will step on others to get it!

I have more trouble with myself than I do with all other people.

Have you ever been in the presence of a group of people who seem to pool all of their ignorance?

Am I right in assuming that there are plenty of schools of knowledge, but, few schools of wisdom?
Wisdom is knowing what to do when you don't know what to do.

I cannot be satisfied with anyone else until I'm satisfied with myself.

I don't like being "talked down to." If those doing the talking to me cannot talk to me as being equal with me, then I really don't care about listening to them.

Some people must have a very large side because all they can see is their own.

Excessive words do not enrich the conversation.
Words are cheap. The wordier, the cheaper.
Action is what really counts, it doesn't come
cheap, but with considerable exertion.
Action is by works; it takes energy and time and has an
expense that goes along with it, however, action gives the
real story. A certain amount of suffering goes with it also.
Action requires determination and effort.

"Supply and demand" dictate the value of ones speech.
Attitude explains one's inward feelings.
Our conversation tells what we are inside.
Visual observation explains what we are on the outside.
Our countenance reflects our inward emotions.

Wisdom is knowledge that is mellowed with longevity.
Wisdom is knowledge that is ripened by maturity.
Wisdom is knowledge seasoned with dedication and determination.
Wisdom is unspoiled knowledge.
Wisdom is knowledge proven through tested experience.
Wisdom is knowledge that is seasoned with common sense.
Wisdom is incubated knowledge.
Wisdom is a symptom of knowledge.

A person may have knowledge without wisdom, but a person cannot have wisdom without knowledge. Conclusion: knowledge must come first.

Not being happy doesn't mean one is miserable.

"He made me mad," no, I allowed myself to become angry, therefore he controls me. I became his slave! Didn't affect him, it only hurts me!

Things that poison me are: hate, bitterness, exaggeration of the truth, my idle talk, my impatience, hypocrisy, and no self discipline.

Tomorrow is governed by today's activities. Tomorrow is built on what we do today.

It can take years to make real good friends, but it only moments to lose them.

Every person that is trying to do right has a full time job without trying to run the life of others.

He who is trustworthy is a good person to know.

A plain "yes" or "no" answer is easily understood and does not require a hundred frivolous words to back it up!

Almost right is wrong.
You cannot help others without helping yourself.
You cannot hurt others without hurting yourself.

In trying to keep up with the Jones's, it costs a person their peace of mind, joy and happiness. If you should catch up with the

Jones's, would it bring happiness and give you peace of mind? It kinda' like space, you'll never run out of Jones's.

The most miserable people are those who strive to impress others.
Funny how I can be more worried about what other people think of me than what God thinks of me.

A person cannot find happiness and peace until they disregard, to a certain extent, what others think.
Other people do not appreciate my efforts to impress them.
Besides, other folks will value me more if I just relax and be myself. They know immediately of my inferior feelings about myself when I am "putting on." Another thing about those who are trying to impress is that they are envious of others.
Pursue your own happiness and peace of mind and be thankful that God has blessed you with what you have.

The reward is removed and appreciation by others is completely gone when a person complains about doing a thing, even though it was a good deed. My complaining only upsets others and makes me unhappy.
By taking all of your grievances to the one that created everything, will accomplish more than complaining to others just like yourself.

October, 1978:
> Summer is past and the leaves begin to rattle, Our trip to the beach got shot out of the saddle.
> The trees are full of color, our hearts are filled with glee, We'll take a trip to the mountains and just forget about the sea

jack joiner

I don't want my thoughts to be herded off in to some direction that a person on the radio or television may be trying to guide my mind into. I would rather my thoughts would be original and centered around my world of living, likes, environment, family and others.

I do not want my mind to be "polluted" with mental trash.

I do not want "trash" singing and "trash" music trying to influence or guide my thinking. I like for my thoughts to be inspirational and not from "junk sounds and idle words."

I do not want to be entertained with idle conversation. I am "ill-at-ease" when someone is trying to pour junk conversation onto me just because of my being in his presence. If a person has nothing to say then I don't want to have to listen to it. [My dad used to say, "when you hear nothing, say nothing"]

Silence is golden, even in the presence of those that I like to be with. The communication is there without being overly-wordy. Just being with those that I care about is great, and lots of conversation is good, when there is love, fellowship, and compassion in what is being said.

The ability to do creative thinking is a God given gift. I do not want to corrupt it with mental pollution.

My mind and time are precious and limited, therefore, I would like to take the greatest advantage of them. I do not want to be robbed of these values by some thoughtless person who has nothing to say except idle words. I do not need to be, nor do I desire to be entertained with complaints, gossip, backbiting, and pessimistic idle words.

Our thoughts would be divinely inspired if we would let them be. It is necessary that I be still, quiet and patient in order to think a matter out.

A minute of thought about God and His creation is worth more than a lifetime of wrong conversation.

All thoughts that their brain produces leaks right out of their mouth.
My suggestion is "don't be one of those."

This is not verbatim, but I like what it means:
> Brilliant people talk about ideas, Average people talk about things.
> Little people talk about people.

I, along with most people that try to do right, would like to be able to say when we get to the end of life: "May it be a better place because I was there."

Don't you just hate to be around folks that pass judgment on every statement that you make? Sure will make you not say as much.

The value of a favor to me is a total loss if you complain about having to do it. Friends do not complain about the privilege of helping each other. I hope that I never make a big issue out of helping others. I appreciate what you do for me only if you don't publicize it just to get recognition. If a person cannot be friendly to me, I'd rather they would not be anything to me.

Don't be critical of the way that I do a thing until you know of a better way!

If there is something that you want that you've never had, then you'll have to do something that you've never done to get it.

I wonder if those who want to listen to loud music all time, are subconsciously trying to drown out their conscience. And if these same ones are trying to avoid receiving the message of direction for their lives that their mind is receiving from the Holy Spirit. If a person is not receiving direction from the Holy Spirit, I wonder who is standing in the way?

It is much harder listening to nothing being said than it is for the one saying it! The speaker is evidently receiving mental therapy, but it places a heavy burden on the very heart of the listener.

Our acquaintances know us by our image and reputation, not our character. Most of the time we don't know the truth about each other. God knows us by our character, not by or reputation. He sees us just exactly as we are. He knows the truth!

Luke 12:15 "A man's life consists not in the abundance of the things which he possesses." God judges me on the ways that I use the resources that he has provided me with! Don't take this too lightly: "we will be judged on what we do with what we have!"

If a person is abused and treated somewhat as a slave during their childhood, then, when they become an adult, they too, will treat others the only way that they know, that is, the way they were treated as a child, because that is their only experience.

Those who do all of their thinking out loud are a tremendous burden on others; it borders on boredom!

Those who are concerned about themselves only, and with little thought given about the good of others are selfish and are very unhappy and unstable. People who serve God by ministering to others find happiness and peace with God.

People's own tongues degrade or upgrade themselves every time they speak. Others determine what you are by your talk. They are impressed or unimpressed by what you say and how you say it.

Many degrade themselves by trying to impress others.

Is adultery in the bed worse than adultery in the head?

Those who exaggerate the truth do not fall short of lying!
Those who do not keep their word, lie.
People who are always late for appointments, fall short of being honest.

Your activities describe your faith.
As your faith is, so goes your life.
Your lifestyle is your faith.
The way you live is evidence of your faith.
You live what you believe.

When I look out across the ocean, I think of myself as being like the wind, the waves and tempest; sometimes I'm up and sometimes I'm down.

When a person is talking too much, and that about unimportant things; then I can't help but believe that they subconsciously are attempting to control my mind.
You are not talking to the right person when you're talking continuously, non-stop, to me about how mean others are to you and how you have more troubles than anyone else. Just be willing to lay your life on the line to the one that can take care of all of your problems.

Folks are not helping you when they're laying all of their aches and pains and problems on you. They're not making you have a desire to be in their presence.

Sometimes it seems to me that most of my opposition comes from those who are supposed to care for me the most

I can't help but feel sorry for people who speak their whole mind all the time; but, my heart goes out to those who have to listen to it.

I guess you too have been in the presence of people who interrupts your conversation to prove their point, even to the extent that you never have the opportunity to express your thoughts. The conversation ends and they walk off thinking that they proved that their views were right and the most important, and that your views had no value. However, I think they lost more than the conversation.

A person is considered grown-up only when he lays aside the ways of his childhood.

It is not what you receive that brings happiness, but what you give.
Giving without receiving has much honor, but giving because you received has little honor.

You are rewarded greatly for your deeds done in secret.

You'll have more credibility with others if you call their name every time that you come in contact with them, and let them express themselves completely without interruption. In normal conversation, the patient listener has more creditability than the person doing all the talking. Again, there is no free speech, you'll pay for it either now or in the hereafter.

I find it difficult for me to give credibility to folks for their good deed if they display a very bad attitude.

Don't get too pre-occupied with things which hinder you from finding time to stop, be still, and listen to the Holy Spirit. It's impossible for me to hear the Holy Spirit when there is idle conversation, loud television, radio, or other unnecessary loud activity taking place.

The true picture can be distorted by words without knowledge. [taken out of context from Job 38:2]

It appears that folks who tell all their problems and complaints to others are seeking pity. Also, people who are sincerely looking for comfort and a way to solve their problems, tell them all to God!

Do some people really think that the "here and now" is everything?

I like good fellowship, conversation and fellowship as well as the next person but, God can do a good job of carrying your burdens and I'm very poor at it.

Many times people are offended at the truth if it's not in their favor.

There are times when people do not speak-up with some truth that needs to be brought out because of offending someone.

One should not complain about not being able to go to sleep until they are willing to stop talking.

The extent of one's peace of mind and happiness is directly related to the depth of relationship a person has with God, and not because of their material possessions.

Have you ever seen a person that, if you don't stop talking while they're interrupting, they'll get louder until you do?
It's fairly difficult to enlighten those who already know everything.

Psychiatrist are right in advising their patients to not hold in the things that trouble them, but let it out; tell someone what's bothering them. The big mistake is not telling them that the only one that they can tell that is capable of helping them is God. Another human does not have the power to fulfill the need: so, why burden them beyond what they can bear? God wants the troubles laid on him, it's a part of showing faith in Him, and a part of his plan. It's not a burden on him, but it's a means of worshiping Him. The sooner a person is able to talk to God in private, about every small or large thing in their life, the sooner they will be restored back to their normal self. Remember, God has already given you all the strength necessary to do a lot of things for yourself. It's also up to us to let him take care of us. We're the only ones that hinders Him from doing the things that He would like to do. God is not limited, we're the only ones that restrict Him. We're in the way of God doing great works within each of us.

There are folks who never judge others by the color of their skin; By the way, did you ever dream in color? If you don't remember, then you haven't.

Fools are known as what they are.
If a person is in good fellowship with God, then they can talk over their problems and burdens with Him and He will honor their requests.

As the Christian gains more faith in God; he gains more confidence in self because the spirit of God is the spirit that is in him.

If you show affection, you receive affection.
If you make yourself loveable, you'll be loved.
Make yourself trustworthy, you'll be trusted.
If you appear to be a slob, you'll be thought of as a slob.

Atheists are not the only ones that are on their way to hell; lost believers are just as lost as atheists! Punishment for lost church members may be more severe because they know about the Lord but fail to seek Him out and fully surrender to Him.

I believe that some, who take on the name of Christ, do so in vain. They ignore the convicting power of the Holy Spirit and will not repent, surrender, and commit their lives to Him. They just console their consciences by telling themselves that they "believe" and or, belong to the church. [They may just have the cart and no horse.]

Proverbs - 16:18 Pride goeth before destruction and a haughty spirit before a fall.

A big majority will follow along with the crowd, whether they're right or wrong, if they as individuals will stand to gain in a monetary way.

Just because a group acts in a mob type manner to take, by whatever force necessary, that which they want, and the law of the land does not interfere, does not make it right anymore than the individual who takes by force to obtain from another individual that which he possesses.

I really like people in general, however, I take a special liking to those who are considerate of others.

Folks have just "gotta" love a person who is willing to drop everything, stop fantasizing, go back to "zero" and stop trying to over-impress.

People will always love you for just being yourself.

A Person's Home Should Be Their Castle

The home should be a place where a person can always go to and find peace, rest and comfort. It should be a place where everyone there loves you and is glad when you get home. A place where you're greeted with a smiling welcome, and where one is always at peace with every one there. The home should be a place where you can discuss the things that interest you, ideas that you have, and things that you are, or want to be involved in. A place where everyone is anxious to help others in the home. This should be accomplished with very sincere efforts by all, and without any arrogance of criticism. It should be a place where things to be done can be discussed in harmony.

All people of the home should have a goal of helping each other in all their interest while showing an "I CARE ATTITUDE."
No one will ever be happy as long as they criticize and use arrogant remarks about practically everything that is said.

Conclusion

Until all unwarranted criticism, arrogance, hate, blame, mistrust, hostility, opposition and contrariness is abolished, "A PERSON'S HOME WILL <u>NOT</u> BE THEIR CASTLE."

There are those who are fighting life and cannot be a blessing to anyone. They just fight, - fight, ---fight, -------fight, --and - fight!
That's the only way they know, it's been in their life since childhood. Now if they could just let go completely of the heavy load of worries and let God handle every situation in their life, they could live quality lives with happiness and peace, and definitely be a blessing to others.

I don't want a person to tell me how much faith in God that they have and how much they know about the bible, when their tongue is too busy spewing out idle gossip about others.

Mistreating of other people, in my opinion, is SIN.

My refusing to do a favor for others when requested, when it would not work a hardship on me, in their opinion would not make me a friend.

Evidently folks who are mistreated, or abused and have an unhappy childhood, or have been raised in a home that was under the "guise" of Christianity seem to think that that's the way they should live and treat all others. I think they will never have peace and happiness until they make an effort to look for the good in life instead of the bad. Stop running the race with the fictitious "JONES." There will never be any happiness until they appreciate that which they have.

If I do not do the things in this life that God wants me to do, then I'm not willing! Because God does not require anything of me that He does not give me the ability to do.

Would people think less of a person if they were kind, good, cheerful, peaceful, friendly and loving, rather than being abusive and hostile?

I like folks that have my interest at heart along with their own. Wouldn't it be great if the normal employee would feel the same way about the person that pays him for his service.

I don't understand how a person can appreciate the Creator if they don't appreciate nature. If they don't appreciate the Creator and His creation, I'm of the opinion that happiness and peace will not come to them until they do.

It seems to me that some people have "missed the boat" on what it takes to be happy.

The tongue is more destructive and causes more hurt and unhappiness than any thing I know.

The sooner a person finds out that they cannot run other people's lives, the better off they'll be. Also, the sooner a person stops carrying the whole world on their shoulders, the better off they'll be.

If some people have eyes for the "rich and famous" only, they will always be most miserable. I firmly believe that having eyes for the poor and people in need, with compassion, will somewhat bring peace of mind and happiness in a person's life.

Some folks are so particular that they cannot enjoy life and cause those around them to be uncomfortable.

Suppose We Lived In
The Land Of Reversia

Wearing the pants of the family doesn't make a man!
The man of the house is not necessarily the man!
If the servant is the ruler, then there could be some serious confusion!

Unpleasant things are made worse and continue to prey on the mind if someone discusses it over and over.

The "painfully perfect" people live miserable lives and cause peaceful people much discomfort.

Adults who pitch a tantrum in order to have things their way, or to get what they want, reminds me of small children who were never properly disciplined. They are selfish and self-centered, with very little respect for others.

The sooner we can forget about what other people think, the sooner we can do our best with much less effort. Others will be much more impressed by our honesty and simplicity, and will appreciate us much more.

A criminal lawyer who obstructs justice is a paid criminal who is protected by our system and honored by the public.

Sometimes I think that every time some people speak, they're attempting to prove themselves right and someone else wrong.

I wonder what the outcome would be if everyone strived as hard to find the good in others as they do to find the bad.

It is far better to say nothing than to say too much.

How can we know how to live if we don't read the Bible????

The mind of a person belongs to them and God. When a person, in good mental health, becomes belligerent, hostile, high tempered, self-centered and (or) arrogant, then God moves out and Satan moves in with a demonic spirit. God will not reside with Satan. He moves completely from the controls of your life and you have unintentionally allowed Satan to become in charge. It happens so smoothly that we're not aware of the transition. Now you have permitted something to happen that you don't even realize. Sometimes we just sit back and enjoy the ride with Satan at the steering wheel of our life and God completely out of the picture. We even think that it feels good and appear to like it for a season until we come to our senses. WAKE UP FOLKS!!! We can wake up if we so desire. It's time to appreciate our God given lives. REVOKE SATAN'S DRIVERS LICENSE, GIVE THE STEERING WHEEL OF YOUR LIFE BACK TO GOD. Forget about selfish feelings, wear a smile. It's the needs that we fulfill in the lives of others, that fills our own soul with peace and happiness.

Some folks use very good judgment Some use common judgment I'm afraid that for some, judgment is yet to come.

There are people that spend their whole lives finding faults in others, but they will never cover them all, neither will they live long enough to cover their own.
As for me, I should never find fault in others until I have overcome my own.

We choose: our attitude whether to smile or frown to be friendly or not enjoy life or not be uptight or relax worship God or earthly possessions help others or only ourselves.

It all boils down to: if we have a mind, we have a choice.

Happiness comes not from the favors I do for self, but for others.

Bitter words of degradation does not make the heart grow fonder.
I cannot get close to a person that degrades me much of the time.
A person is degrading me when they can only speak of my faults.

If you hate a person bad enough, you can easily find fault with everything that they do or say, and can easily blame them with all things that are not to your liking.

Hard work will not hide a bad attitude.

If I only worried about the things that God was unable to take care of, then I wouldn't have a worry at all.

If a picture is worth a thousand words, a smile is worth much more.

ATTITUDE

(some food for thought)

A person with a bad attitude will have very few friends.

A good attitude by a spouse will make a good home.

A bad attitude by a spouse will wreck a home.

Just because a person does not feel good does not give them a right to have a bad attitude toward others. (ouch)

Attitude is an option.

A person chooses to have a bad or good attitude.

It's a pleasure to be in the presence of person with a good attitude.

It's a pain to be with a person with a bad attitude.

A homely looking person is pretty if they have a good attitude A beautiful person is ugly if they have a bad attitude.

Whether people like you or not depends on your attitude.

People like to be with people with a good attitude.

I don't know why some folks choose to have a bad attitude.

Not having your way gives you no right to have a bad attitude.

Our whole life depends on our attitude.

Others judge us by our attitude.

Our attitude seems to be the most important part about us.

Some people have a good attitude around folks they like.

Then, some have a bad attitude around people they don't like.

You cannot hide your attitude.

A bad attitude can and will affect your health and longevity of life.

The amount of friends is governed by our attitude.

Each attitude is governed by the individual.

No one has a right to have a bad attitude just because they don't feel good.

A good attitude makes a person very attractive.

A bad attitude makes a person unattractive.

A good attitude reflects the love of God.

A bad attitude reflects an evil mind.

Attitude is the most important resource available to man.

A bad attitude is a curse on an individual.

Others don't deserve to be treated by someone with a bad attitude.

A good attitude is enjoyed very much by others.

Our attitude is reflected by the expression on our face.

It is quite difficult to have compassion on someone with a bad attitude.

It appears to be easy for a person with a bad attitude to be contrary.

A person's attitude unveils their feelings.

A person's attitude tells the condition of the soul.

Could it be that a hypochondriac does not have a good attitude?

A person with a bad attitude appears to hate.

A person with a good attitude is normally compassionate.

A poor attitude is a good foundation to hate.

I love people with a good attitude.

I "strive" to love those who have a poor attitude.

Having a good attitude is a "favor from God."

People with a poor attitude are unhappy.

A person with a poor attitude cost others their peace of mind.

Poor attitude and poor personality go hand in hand.

Folks with a bad attitude will not listen to instructions.

A poor attitude is not an excuse for not having a good attitude.

Gratitude is reflected by a person's attitude.

A poor attitude is not a divine inspiration.

Nothing seems to please a person who has a bad attitude.

Let's face it, a person who always has a poor attitude, needs help.

1. A bad attitude is not offset by doing lots of hard work.
2. Is one of the most important things in life.
3. Makes you a success or failure.
4. Makes friends or drives them away.
5. A good attitude is of God.

6. If a bad attitude is not of God, then who is it from?
7. Bad attitudes is the foundation for unhappy marriages.
8. Bad attitude hinders progress.
9. Bad attitude kills sexual desires.
10. A good attitude makes homely looking people look pretty.
11. Never sit in the drive's seat until you earn it and are qualified.

****

Different Subject:

Give freely to others before they give unto you.

Do more than is expected of you, it will not go unrewarded.

Do for others before they do for you.

Do for others while there is time to do so, there will come a time when it's too late.

Search for opportunities to fulfill the needs of others, it's very rewarding.

Live for the thrill of doing for others for no compensation.

****

THE BITTER TRUTH

Some where along the line many people have
"missed the boat."
All along life's way as we all observe the ways of
much of the population that we encounter each
day, it is noticeable that little respect is shown for
the other person.

Who do we think that we are?
How do we think that we got here?
What about this life that is in us?
What is the purpose of our being?
Who do we think creates a human body?
Who is living in this created body?
Who is doing our thinking?

How Much Of A Hypocrite Are We? Understanding Ones Own Christian Life

1. Am I a peace maker or trouble maker?
2. Am I considered to be a light in my community?
3. Do I get angry at others without cause?
4. Do I carry hate in my mind for some one?
5. Will I go to my grave hating someone?
6. If I offend someone do I apologies even though I'm not wrong?
7. Do I use God's name in vain even to express myself?
8. Do I try to justify myself without considering if I'm wrong?
9. Do I make snap judgments without even thinking about it?
10. Do I consider myself only when judging other?
11. Do I rudely interrupt others just to have my say?
12. Do I hold a grudge? (It's only detrimental to my health).
13. Am I jealous of those having a better lifestyle than me?
14. Do I feel superior to those not as fortunate as I?
15. Am I really thankful to those who are responsible for my lifestyle?
16. Do I hate those who offend me rather than forgiving them?
17. Do I speak ill of those who don't do it my way?
18. If I have hate in my heart, am I evil?
19. Will it affect my health if I am housing hate in my heart?
20. Do I greet only the people that I'm familiar with?

21. Do I attend church to worship god and have christian fellowship only?
22. Am I only interested in doing good if others can have knowledge of it?
23. Am I interested more in what movie actors are doing than in what god's people are doing?
24. Do I forgive others who offend me and not hold a grudge?
25. Do I do things just to be seen of others?
26. Do I have to tell others of something good that I did for someone else.
27. Am I rewarded for telling others about my righteousness?
28. Do I think that God is as pleased with my life as I am pleased with it?
29. Am I sure that I'm headed in the right direction with my life?
30. Will the unforgiveness in my heart be acceptable at the end?
31. Do I profane the good name of others just because of jealousness?
32. Am I a backbiter except when facing others?
33. Do I purposely speak detrimental words of other people that I don't like?
34. Am I really living the life that I think that god is pleased with?
35. Am I more friendly to those who have more than to others?
36. Do I only see the faults of others when I have the same or worse?
37. Am I appreciative and show love to my family members?
38. Am I known as a smiler or a frowner?
39. Does it show that I love myself most by demanding that everything be my way?

40. Do I respect the opinion of others without being critical of them?
41. Am I judgmental of all others?
42. Do I really believe that broad is the way that leads to destruction?
43. Do I really believe that narrow is the way to eternal life and few find it?
44. Do I believe that every one that says lord, lord will enter heaven?
45. Is my church membership going to save me?
46. Will my bible study save me in the end?
47. Does my salvation depend on doing the will of the father that is in heaven?
48. Will I be known as a foolish person if I do not do the will of God?
49. If sometimes I have foolish thoughts, will I be considered good enough?
50. Will I be known as a freak or fanatic if I try to live by the teachings of the bible?
51. Do I bore others with my bragging on myself?. I would have gotten scolded and shamed by my parents if I ever boasted. Besides, I think it's very rude of a person to brag on them self.

(these are thoughts that came to mind when reading Matt: chapters 5, 6 seven)

I'm sure that all these questions dwell in the minds of every human that is living and has ever lived.

The truth is that we are all created by God. He has put his own life in each us and has given us free reign over the way that we live and the way that we treat Him. We are guided by the spirit of God that lives within each of us.

We also have the choice of listening to him as he guides us through our choice of good and evil. He is there directing our every decision in what we should do and what we should not do; however, we have a choice of doing what he is telling us to do or to quench the thought. Sometimes it does not appear to be in our plans to adhere to what our conscience is telling us. I'm sure that we all question what our conscience is telling us from time to time.

Let's face it, God is leading the way whether we like it or not. He will never lead us in the wrong way. He loves us and will always guide us. I know that the way He leads us is always the right way to go.

God Is Our Conscience And Lives In Our Minds.

He is always there and lives there every moment of our life. LISTEN TO HIM. We cannot hear him or be guided by him if we are listening to loud secular music or being entertained by TV. We are pushing him aside when we do not take time to just be quiet and listen to what He is putting into our thoughts. If God is not directing your mind, it would be good if you did something about it. If you are not treating others as you would treat God, then you had better give some serious thinking because the life that is in you is the same God that is in them. He created each of us and put His own life in all. So, if we are not good to others then we are not good to our Maker. If we go about fulfilling the needs of others, then we are doing the same for God. If we mistreat others, even if we think they deserve it, we're mistreating the God that gave us life in the first place. That which He has created is his "handy work" and when we disrespect His created, we are slamming God and shutting him out of our life.

We ask ourselves, "WHAT'S WRONG WITH ME, I'VE READ THE BIBLE MANY TIMES AND DO SO ALMOST DAILY. I GO TO CHURCH AND LISTEN TO THE PREACHER AND ENJOY THE GOOD MUSIC AND SINGING, YET NOTHING SEEMS TO BE GOING RIGHT IN MY LIFE. LORD, WHAT ARE YOU DOING IN MY LIFE ? ? ?"

Folks, it's not what God is doing in our lives, it's what we're doing in and with our lives. Are we living for others as well as for ourselves? (OUCH) Are we downing others to make them look bad in order to make ourselves look good comparatively speaking? Are we asking: "GOD, WHAT SHOULD I DO IN THIS CASE?" Are we treating others as God Himself in His created? ? ? ? Are we continually looking for ways to help someone in need and that without compensation, praise or to be seen by others? When we fulfill the needs of others, do we do it with a pleasant countenance on our face, and count it a blessing to be able to do something for someone in need? Happiness comes from helping others, without it there is no happiness. If we truly love God, we love all others, though we may not like their ways.

Why is it that I sometimes think that God ought to be answering my prayers of request?
Well, to start with, God has given to me strength, knowledge, wisdom, patience, time and the know how to do the things that I am requesting Him to do for me.
It finally comes to my mind that I am the servant and not the opposite. God provides me adequately if I would only look around and observe the many ways that He provides for his own creation. If I would only recognize things that I take for granted that He has already done, and is continually doing. I would see that I'm being well taken care of by His Grace,

COULD THERE BE MORE TO LIFE THAN I, ME AND MINE?

THE WAY A PERSON ACTS TOWARD OTHERS IS THE WAY GOD SEES THEM ACTING TOWARD HIM.

THE WAY A PERSON TALKS ABOUT OTHERS IS THE WAY GOD HEARS THEM TALKING ABOUT HIM.

WHEN A PERSON GOSSIPS ABOUT ANOTHER PERSON THEY ARE GOSSIPING ABOUT A GOD CREATED CREATURE; THEREFORE THEY ARE SINNING AGAINST GOD.

WHEN A PERSON IS RUDE TO SOMEONE,
THAT PERSON IS BEING RUDE TO
GOD,BELIEVE IT OR NOT.

WHEN A PERSON STEALS FROM SOMEONE
ELSE THEY ARE STEALING FROM GOD.

WHEN A PERSON DOES NOT DO THE WORK
HE IS PAID TO DO THAT'S STEALING. YOU
KNOW THE REST OF THE STORY.

WHEN A PERSON THINKS THAT THEY ARE
BETTER THAN OTHERS, THEY SHOULD TAKE
A GOOD LOOK AT THEM SELF BECAUSE THEY
ARE NOW THINKING THAT THEY ARE BETTER
THAN A PERSON THAT GOD CREATED.

WHATEVER WE DO, (OR) DON'T DO FOR
OTHERS, WE'RE DOING THE SAME TO
GOD. (BIBLE SCRIPTURE TO CONFIRM
THIS: MATT., 25: vs. 40 AND vs. 45.)

A person is as big as the things that make them angry.

As the service goes, so goes the business.

Almost right is wrong.

Make your job important, it will return the favor.

Nothing improves one's hearing more than praise.

The largest room in the world is the room for improvement.

A minute of thought is worth an hour of talk.

Having an itch for something does not get it done, you have to scratch for it.

You cannot help those in need without helping yourself.

We have an outward countenance that expresses our inner emotions.

****

I believe that God gives to each of us a mental picture of our disobedience and also a vision of what will come upon us if we continue to be disobedient. I believe that He will teach us a lesson that we will never forget if we don't take Him seriously when He gives us these premonitions.

Some folks don't understand the ability of others when they say the same things over and over again or go into too much detail about simple things.

Good friends are made by a good attitude, not by a person's financial worth.

THINK ABOUT THIS:
IS SATAN GETTING THE VICTORY OVER ME BY ROBBING ME OF LIFE'S HAPPINESS???????

"If complaining was profitable there would be many rich people."

LET GOD SPEAK THROUGH HIS PEOPLE:

The loud mouths of this country appear to be in control of how we live. (The saying "the squeaking wheel gets the grease.")

****

Creating humor is better than creating a problem.

****

COULD THIS BE THE WAY SOME THINK?

My ways are always right, why should I consider the feelings of others?

Why should I be nice to people, there is nothing in it for me?
(oh yes there is)

Why should I smile, no one smiles at me? (well, guess what.)
Why should I be considerate of others, I don't owe them anything.

Why am I never rewarded for the many things that I do, I tell everybody about my good works. I also tell all my problems to others but still they don't do anything about them.

Many people have many problems but don't want to burden others with them unless there is something that they can help with.

****

I had rather be at hard work than be in the presence of a person with a bad attitude.

" DO FOR OTHERS BEFORE THEY DO FOR YOU."

I most always have pains but I don't have to be one!

I like the words "attitude adjustment," it should be used more often.

Hard work does not off set a bad attitude.

Is my life a stepping stone for others, or, am I a stumbling stone?

The type of life that a person lives determines their destiny. Even though they appear to be just normal, they could miss Heaven by not living by the will of God. (matt. 7: 21)

One cannot be a continuous fault finder of others and have fellowship with God.

Unless mentally or physically incompetent, every one person should be responsible for the results from their words or actions.

A person cannot love God without loving his children.
One cannot hate others and have peace with God. If they say that they have peace with God, they are only fooling themselves.

If a person really wants to be unhappy, they could let their conversation and mind dwell on unpleasant things. Frankly I prefer the opposite.

****

AN OLDIE BUT GOODIE THAT LIVES ON:

GOD GRANT ME THE SERENITY TO ACCEPT
THE THINGS THAT I CANNOT CHANGE, THE
COURAGE TO CHANGE THE THINGS I CAN, AND
THE WISDOM TO KNOW THE DIFFERENCE.

****

Doing me a favor with a bad attitude is not a favor at all.

If I expect courteous results, I have to use diplomacy not rudeness.

Contrary to what some may think, when one complements another person, they're actually being complimented in the eyes of the listener.

****

THE HUMAN MIND It can be filled with worry, or it can be filled with joy and peace.

It can contain many negatives, or it can have very positive thinking.

It can contain a lot of junk, or filled with the love of God.

It can be filled with a bad attitude, or a very pleasant personality.

It has a choice of much hate, or filled with lots of compassion.

It can be full of a selfish attitude, or a personality of serving where needed.

It can be filled with other people's business, or it may be more concerned with it's own.

It can be loaded with worldly things, or filled with the love of God, but not both.

****

If you worry, don't pray. If you pray, don't worry.

****

The longer I live, the more I realize the impact of attitude on life. Attitude is sometime more important than what is being said.

It is more important than the past, than education,, than money, than circumstances, than failures, than successes, what people think of say or do. It is more important than appearance, giftedness or skill.
It will break a company --- a church ---a home!

The remarkable thing is we have a choice every day regarding the attitude we will embrace for that day. We cannot change our past...we cannot change the inevitable. The only thing that we can do is play on the one string we have, and that is our attitude!

To quote Charles Swindall: "I am convinced that life is 10% what happens to me and 90% how I react to it. And so it is with you...
we are all in charge of our ATTITUDES."

****

IT IS, BY FAR, BETTER TO KEEP YOUR MOUTH SHUT AND LET PEOPLE THINK YOU TO BE LESS THAN INTELLIGENT THAN TO OPEN IT AND BLESS THEM WITH THE FACT!

I BELIEVE THAT:

1. A person misses 99% of Gods blessings when they are in a hurry.
2. God hears a patient person's prayers.
3. God does not honor an impatient person's prayers.
4. God does not bless a person when they're complaining about worldly things, and possibly, may not bless those who are complaining about anything.
5. God honors the people who spend time with him in reading
6. His word and praying earnestly, such as a little child desiring something from his mother and daddy.
7. That God could and would heal most of our infirmities if we would be totally consecrated to him, obedient to his word, be patient, and consider Him personally the most important thing in our life.

How can people that talk all the time think that they know more than the folks that listen, think and read?

I suppose that people that have everything their way all time think that maybe they are smarter than others. Beside that, by having things their way all time does not make them happy, but brings sorrow in the end, plus brings misery to a lot of other people.

Insecure people will always try to dominate the conversation.

Words that soak into your ears are whispered, not yelled.

Forgive your enemies, it messes up their heads.

Big grudges are normally carried by "little" people.

You cannot unsay a cruel word.

The best sermons are lived, not preached.

Remember silence is sometimes the best answer.

The biggest troublemaker that you will ever have to deal with watches you from the mirror every morning.

Good judgment comes from experience from bad judgment.

Someone has said live simply, love generously, care deeply, speak kindly and don't worry about the rest.

I find that the more that I dwell on a problem, the more of a problem it becomes.

Did you ever know a person that wants to just wallow around in their own self pity?

It's not such a bad world after all, it's the people.

I feel that folks that have to have their own way all time has a problem with their relationship with God.

Folks that are ignorant don't know it.

Wasted time can never be recovered.

Missed opportunities for a person to do for others who are in need is a blessing missed.

Just because I don't talk about my aches and pains, don't think that I don't have my share of them.

If you are looking for gloom and doom you can find it on every corner plus you'll find plenty of audience who want to chat with you about it.
If you're looking for peace then look in the right places and you'll find peace.

A person should not be critical of another's faults until he corrects his own.

LORD, I HAVE A PROBLEM, IT'S ME.

By: *Jack Joiner*